RUNNING FOR BEGINNERS

RUNNING FOR BEGINNERS

THE EASIEST GUIDE TO RUNNING YOUR FIRST 5K IN ONLY 6 WEEKS

ACHIEVE MORE IN RUNNING SERIES

JOHN MCDONNELL

First published in 2023 by Greative Books Publishing, Ltd.

Grogey Road

Fivemiletown

Tyrone

BT750NT

Copyright © 2023 by John McDonnell

The moral right of the author has been asserted

All rights reserved.

No part of this book may be reproduced in any form or by any electronic or mechanical means, including information storage and retrieval systems, without written permission from the author, except for the use of brief quotations in a book review.

ISBN Paperback: 979-8-3728-4540-4

CONTENTS

Disclaimer	xi
About Your Coach	xiii
Introduction	xv
Personal 1-To-1 Coaching	xix
1. A SPECIAL INVITATION TO JOIN ACHIEVE ONLINE RUNNING CLUB	1
2. BENEFITS OF RUNNING	3
3. WHAT IT TAKES	6
4. THE PROGRAM EXPLAINED	9
5. FORM AND TECHNIQUE	14
6. DYNAMIC EXERCISES	18
7. POST WORKOUT STRETCHING	20
8. NUTRITION, HYDRATION & SLEEP	23
9. HOW SHOULD IT FEEL	25
What to do if you experience pain	26
10. 6 WEEK PROGRAM	28
11. WEEK 1	29
Session 1 (Day 1)	29
Session 2 (Day 2)	32
Session 3 (Day 3)	34
12. WEEK 2	36
Session 1 (Day 4)	37
Session 2 (Day 5)	38
Session 3 (Day 6)	40

13. WEEK 3	42
Session 1 (Day 7)	43
Session 2 (Day 8)	45
Session 3 (Day 9)	46
14. WEEK 4	48
Session 1 (Day 10)	49
Session 2 (Day 11)	50
Session 3 (Day 12)	51
15. WEEK 5	53
Session 1 (Day 13)	54
Session 2 (Day 14)	55
Session 3 (Day 15)	56
16. WEEK 6	58
Session 1 (Day 16)	59
Session 2 (Day 17)	60
5k Day (Day 18)	61
17. 8 WEEK PROGRAM	64
18. WEEK 1	65
Session 1 (Day 1)	65
Session 2 (Day 2)	69
19. WEEK 2	71
Session 1 (Day 3)	72
Session 2 (Day 4)	73
20. WEEK 3	75
Session 1 (Day 5)	75
Session 2 (Day 6)	77
21. WEEK 4	79
Session 1 (Day 7)	80
Session 2 (Day 8)	82

22. WEEK 5	84
Session 1 (Day 9)	85
Session 2 (Day 10)	86
23. WEEK 6	88
Session 1 (Day 11)	89
Session 2 (Day 12)	90
24. WEEK 7	92
Session 1 (Day 13)	93
Session 2 (Day 14)	94
25. WEEK 8	96
Session 1 (Day 15)	96
5k Day (Day 16)	98
26. WHAT'S NEXT	100
What is Parkrun?	101
Congratulations	103
Also by John McDonnell	105
Appendix I - Bodyweight Workout	125

DISCLAIMER

Keeping physically active is key to maintaining a healthy lifestyle. But it is always best to check with your doctor before taking on a sport like running to ensure it is safe for you to do so. Although this program eases new runners into the sport gently, please ensure you get clearance from your doctor.

ABOUT YOUR COACH

My name is John McDonnell and I've been a UK Athletics Coach in Running Fitness since 2015. During the past eight years I've worked with hundreds of beginner runners in addition to more seasoned runners looking to get into top racing condition. I have a passion for the sport and there is nothing I like better than to see a new runner find that self-belief and go on to complete their first 5k. I have great pride in my runners who continue on in the sport to complete longer distances and go on to take huge satisfaction in their running lives. The sport has been incredibly beneficial to me and to the quality of my life and I enjoy passing this passion along to my athletes. I hope you find that spark and ignite a love for the sport that I know will encourage a better life for yourself.

As for myself, I started running back in 2010, when I completed my first 5k. Since then I have competed in over 30 marathons including two world majors. I have coached new runners from the age of 8 up to 80 and have enjoyed working with everyone. Trust me, you can do this! I've seen the most unlikely people run their first 5k and go on to tackle a marathon within two years. I'm not saying you need to run marathons. Let's get through the 5k first. But you never know what the future holds once you complete that first 5k.

INTRODUCTION

I will start with why I personally got into coaching. It was back in 2013, when I was into my third year of running. I just ran my third marathon of the year, in my first year of marathon running. I finished the race, made my way back to my hotel, took a shower, grabbed my bags, checked out and began the 5 hour drive back home. I had to cross the course I had just run at a point about a mile from the finish line. In doing so, I saw a woman still running out on the course. It must have been about 6 hours after the start. She didn't look like what most people would call a runner. Like me from a couple of years before, she was overweight and appeared out of shape. She was running slowly and seemed to be in a great deal of pain. It was warm out and I knew she was struggling. Yet, she continued, putting one foot in front of the other. Obviously, she wasn't out of shape. She completed the first 25 miles and was still going forward.

This really spoke to me. I was so impressed by this person's grit and determination. I wanted to have these qualities. I ran the marathon as well, but this individual showed me what it meant to be a runner. It was at this point I decided that becoming a running coach was for me. Not to persuade people to run marathons, but to help people accomplish something they may have never thought possible. Running is for everyone, of every age, shape, size, and ability.

So you want to be a runner. Or maybe you were a runner and you would like to be one again. The good news is that if it is something you really want to do, it can be done. As a matter of fact, with either this eight week, or the six week program, not only can it be done, but it is really straight forward.

What will running your first 5k feel like? It will feel amazing! If this is your first 5k the feeling will be indescribable. For me, and so many of the runners I've trained, it was life changing, completely transformational. Most beginners are full of self doubt, but with these programs the progress is gradual. It slowly builds confidence, until one session, it just feels possible. Then, when the graduation run takes place, there is no more room for doubt. You got this!

I recommend getting a training partner or a small

group who will do this with you. Running is not only easier to do in a small group, but the results of a beginner 5k program is greatly improved by having someone or some people to hold each other accountable. You are less likely to skip out on a session, and subsequently lose momentum, if you know someone is counting on you to join them. There is also the added benefit of having someone to celebrate progress and success with as you go.

I am eager to hear about your experience as you progress through this plan and you can provide feedback, questions and overall comments here at 5K Plan Feedback.

PERSONAL 1-TO-1 COACHING

Some runners need that extra little push in order to stay true to their plans. Someone to hold them accountable. Someone to adjust their plans when injuries and niggles start appearing. Someone to answer questions on a daily or weekly basis and explain the ins-and-outs of the training. I work with runners of every ability starting with the complete beginner, all for less than the price of your daily coffee.

Discover a personalized approach to elevate your running journey with my coaching services. Embrace a monthly coaching package featuring comprehensive support: receive weekly training updates, engage in regular video call check-ins, and access unlimited guidance to address all your inquiries and worries. While books and guides provide valuable insights, nothing parallels the impact of individualized coaching. Benefit from tailored training plans geared towards specific races or maintaining peak performance between events.

Moreover, within these coaching packages, you'll discover choices for strength training regimens and personalized meal plans. Running holds transformative power, and these all-encompassing coaching packages aim to sculpt you into the well-rounded athlete you aspire to be. Explore your diverse coaching options today at https://jmruncoach.com/services.

If you are ready to elevate your running and crush new personal records then sign up today. Or you can also reach out to me at John McDonnell Running Coach on Facebook and we can discuss your goals and how I can help you reach them. I am also contactable by email at john@jmruncoach.com.

CHANCE TO WIN A MONTH OF FREE PERSONAL COACHING

I am offering everyone who reads this book an opportunity to win one-month of free one-to-one running coaching. Take a look in the Congratulations Chapter at the end of this book to see how to be in with a good chance of winning and making the most of your new sport.

CHAPTER 1
A SPECIAL INVITATION TO JOIN ACHIEVE ONLINE RUNNING CLUB

I HAVE BEEN the head coach at three different running clubs over the years. It has been an absolute privilege to help runners begin their running lives and to play a part in their improvement in the sport over time. I don't think there is anything more satisfying for a coach than to see athletes achieve their goals. That is why I've started Achieve Running Club, an online running club dedicated to bringing people along in our sport.

This is your personal invitation to join our community, for free, and get the support all runners need. I will be personally moderating the Facebook group and checking in from time to time. All your running related questions answered by like minded and knowledgeable runners. All your running related worries put to rest. Be as active or as quiet as you would like. But it would be great to see photos of your achievements, no matter how big or small you may think they are. Every positive experience is another step into your running life and an inspiration to others following in your footsteps. Even the tough days bring something to the table, so share those as well and I'm sure the rest of the community will benefit.

There will also be a regular newsletter emailed out with tips, advice, discounts, and sharing the successes of our members.

Please get involved. It will help you become the runner you always wanted to be. Use the hashtag #AchieveRC in your social media posts and together let's build this community.

How To Join

Website: Achieve Running Club - When you sign up online you will receive a free printable 8 week running journal in PDF format.

Facebook: Achieve Running Club

CHAPTER 2
BENEFITS OF RUNNING

IF YOU HAVE NEVER BEEN a runner, but you see people of all ages, shapes and sizes running around your town or village you may have asked yourself, "why would people do that?" It seems like a funny thing for anyone to *enjoy* doing. But the fact is, for many of us runners, the benefits are so amazing that we couldn't imagine going without it.

As I mentioned in the introduction, for me running started as a method to lose weight. It turned out to be amazingly successful. The more I ran, the more dedicated I was to improving. The more I improved, the more I focussed on making better nutritional choices. It has turned into a complete lifestyle change and one that quite literally saved my life. You can read more about that if you're interested, in my book, "A Heart for Running: How Running Saved My Life" or by looking at my website at https://aheartforrunning.com. That said, running helps burn calories, and when combined with healthy eating choices, is an extremely effective form of exercise to include in a weight-loss regime.

Now, not everyone starts exercise to reduce weight or get into better shape, but for many that is the case. For those of us who are looking to do so, running has been proven to be quite beneficial. According to a number of scientific studies, aerobic exercises, running being a particularly effective one, can reduce stomach fat. It has also been shown that running can help regulate hunger. Of course, this is important in the weight loss circle, but it also encourages a healthier diet. As we all know, weight loss is more highly impacted by what is done in the kitchen than what is done in the gym. So by creating better eating habits, assisted by a good running routine, weight loss is much more easily achieved.

Other studies have shown that running can help maintain a healthy heart and increase your lifespan. It has also been shown to help improve the quality of your sleep, which in turn, helps you to function better during the day. Now who doesn't want to experience these things?

In addition to a healthy body, running has been proven to have significant benefits to your mental health. For one thing, it can help reduce stress and help maintain a young mind by improving learning and memory. There has also been evidence of a reduction to the risk of dementia and other neurological conditions.

Running can be done on your own, with a partner or in a group. One way or the other, it can be of social benefit as well. If you run with a partner or in a group, these social benefits are obvious. You have the opportunity to spend some time with friends and like-minded people, converse about everything life throws at you. Even as a lone-runner, you have that shared experience with other runners to talk about. Runners in general are well known as strong, generous and supportive people and by joining their ranks you are taking a huge step forward in your social life.

Lastly, running is also linked to benefits for those suffering from depression and low mood. I never met a runner who has come back and didn't feel better about life after a run. The half hour or more of alone time can be extremely therapeutic. Just you, the road and some headspace to work through life's difficult issues. There is nothing better.

A healthier body, an improved social life, a clear mind and a longer, better quality of life; who could ask for anything more?

CHAPTER 3
WHAT IT TAKES

WHAT DOES it take to be a runner? Everybody can run and enjoy the activity. If you are an able-bodied person, you can run. There is inspiration all around you. Running isn't easy, but it doesn't have to be the hardest thing you ever do either. So what does it take to become a runner? Start with your why. Why do you want to become a runner? Only you can answer this question. If your reason is clear and you have a strong enough purpose, the *becoming* part is easy. You will dig down and do the work. Otherwise, it will be more difficult, but still possible. There is a great question to ask yourself, "how bad do I want it?" Are you willing to put in the hard work up front for a lifetime of benefits? For me, I began running in order to lose weight. Within the first 2 years of running, I lost over 50lbs. If your *why* is strong enough, you will make no excuses.

Secondly, a small amount of time. This is relative, but it will take no more than three hours per week. We can all find 3 hours in a week that has 168 hours in total. Some weeks will require less, others slightly more.

Lastly, some basic running kit should be acquired, if it isn't already available. Comfortable running shoes, and not necessarily expensive, top of the line racing shoes. A standard trainer that is comfortable to run in will be perfectly suitable. Your feet may swell a little while running so it is advisable to go for something a half size larger than normal. It's best to have a little wiggle room at the front of the shoe.

- A phone with a stopwatch on it or an actual stopwatch (anything that can count minutes and seconds will do).
- Either shorts or leggings, whatever you are most comfortable wearing
- A high-viz vest to be seen while out on the roads or footpaths. It's always best to be seen.
- Women should invest in a good sports bra as this will make running pain free, more comfortable and limit movement.
- A technical top, any running t-shirt should do. Avoid cotton t-shirts as they can chafe and absorb sweat. The key to training in cold weather is to layer up. As you warm up, it is

best to have the option of removing layers as opposed to overheating.
- Possibly a waterproof jacket (this is optional as skin is already waterproof)
- A hat & gloves, depending on the climate

There are a few more optional items that you may find helpful and these will be discussed as we go. Things like a training journal, foam roller, maybe a yoga mat. Nothing elaborate or expensive and you can easily work with what you've got as far as these optional items are concerned.

It takes a small commitment of time, money and hard work. That is all. If you are willing to put those three ingredients together, your life will be immeasurably enhanced. If that sounds OK, then let's go, you got this!

For a list of recommended optional items to get you going, please see recommended items. Again, these things are completely optional, but may make it easier to get through the program.

CHAPTER 4
THE PROGRAM EXPLAINED

THIS IS a six week beginner runner program. I developed this many years ago as a UK Athletics Coach in Running Fitness. There have been hundreds, even thousands, of new runners who have successfully completed this exact program. Over the next six weeks we'll work on developing good running form, breathing techniques and slowly build up your endurance. Each week I will introduce a different coaching point that I will ask you to focus on as you go. None of these are overly technical and everything will be made to be as easy as possible.

You are stronger than you think. The human body is an amazing piece of engineering. The great thing about a six week plan like this is that it is slow enough that it isn't intimidating, but it is still only six weeks. You will be done and running 5k's before you know it. As the weeks go by, and they will fly by, you will gain confidence and self-belief. Report your progress on our website at 5k plan feedback as well as on our Facebook Page at Achieve Running Club.

One thing I would caution against is jumping ahead. Each session is deliberately planned for a specific reason. Although you may very well be fit to do more than what is being asked of you, it isn't worth the risk. It is easy to become discouraged and what we are trying to do is build confidence and self-belief. Stick with the proven plan and it will work. You will run your 5k.

To begin with, this is about completing the distance. It is not to complete the distance in a fast time, or even a specific time. We will get you through your first 5k, lay down a marker, and then you can work on improving that. As a matter of fact, I have a number of different running improvement books which you can use to improve your times, increase your distances and become a more advanced runner. For now, we are going to get the first 5k done.

Ideally, when doing this program, you will want to find some quiet roads, a park, some forestry trails, anywhere that provides a flat course. It can be on a track or a small loop somewhere. It certainly doesn't have to be a complete 5k route. The idea is that you will be walking and running at different intervals. You will start with walking more and running less until it gradually swings the other way, until we finish by completing the sessions without walking at all.

Each session will start with a brisk walk warm-up, followed by some dynamic exercises. This will get your body ready for the main session. By warming up the muscles and getting the cardio system activated you will find the session goes by just that little bit easier and with less of a risk of an injury. Then you will complete the designated session which will then be followed up with some stretching exercises. As we move through the weeks, there will be a cool down added between the session and the stretching. I will have links to videos to show each of the dynamics and stretches for each of the running sessions.

Try to keep a consistent schedule. You will need three days per week, ideally with at least a day rest in between each session. So something like this:

Session 1 - Monday
Session 2 - Wednesday
Session 3 - Saturday
Or
Session 1 - Tuesday
Session 1 - Thursday
Session 1 - Sunday

If this doesn't work out and you need to do sessions back to back, you will still get this done. But your body makes best use of your workouts when you give it time to rest. Our bodies grow stronger in running, and any other physical activity, through a cycle called adaptation. We workout and challenge our bodies, which breaks down muscle tissue. With good nutrition and rest the body builds back the muscle fibres just that little bit stronger than they were. Then we challenge the body once again. This is why we need good, protein rich foods and plenty of quality sleep.

There is also an eight week plan included, for those who can only dedicate 2 days per week to fitting in a session. Both programs will work quite well and you choose whichever one works best with your schedule.

The main session will be listed as a number of sets x number of repetitions and will consist of a set period of recovery walks between sets.

- A Repetition (or rep) is the number of times you do the activity - in our case it will be a walk or a run
- A Set is the number of times you do a specified number of reps.
- An example is 2 sets x 5 reps 30 seconds run with 90 seconds recovery and 2 minutes recovery between sets.
- This means you run for 30 seconds then walk for 90 seconds and do that 5 times.

- Then after the 5th run that is 1 set complete. You now walk for 2 minutes
- Then another set of 5 of the same 30 seconds run and 90 seconds walking and you are done.
- This is a total of 10 repetitions.

The recovery portion of the session should be when you walk between reps of running. Try to get your breath back as close to normal resting breathing as possible. Big deep, slow breaths work best. There is usually a longer recovery period between two sets allowing you to take on a second set of reps.

There are two things that we will be changing to make improvements. Each week we will either be running for a longer period of time or walking for a shorter period of time. It will slowly transition to the point that eventually, you will be able to run, non-stop, for the full 5k distance without taking any walking breaks.

If you are interested in doing additional work to make this program a little easier, I highly recommend adding some bodyweight workouts. It doesn't take a huge commitment, even 10-20 minutes a few times per week will go a long way. I will put a handy bodyweight plan in Appendix I.

CHAPTER 5
FORM AND TECHNIQUE

WE ARE ALMOST ready to get started with our first week of training. Let's first talk a little bit about form and technique. First and foremost, pace is going to be the biggest key to this whole journey. As I mentioned in the previous chapter, this is going to be about finishing the distance, not about time. You will need to run comfortably. This means slow. **If you are struggling with your breathing, you are going too fast.** I can't stress that enough, so I'll say it again. **If you are struggling with your breathing, you are going too fast.** For some of you this will mean going slightly faster than a walk. Others may find it fairly easy to go at a quicker pace, but this is an individual journey, you don't have to keep up with anyone else.

If you have a training partner(s), you should both/all go at the pace of the slowest runner. Encourage each other, support each other. Like I said earlier, we are going to finish the distance and worry about improving speed later. The earliest sessions should feel easy, almost too easy.

For running form, you want to run *tall*. This means you want to have a good upright posture. We will work on each of these throughout the program, but here are the coaching points I'll be looking to introduce to your running form.

- You have a balloon on a string tied to the base of your skull at the back of your neck, pulling you up from that point - Running Tall
- Shoulders should be relaxed and positioned back and down in relation to your torso
- Imagine you have a bowl of water between your hips and don't want to spill the water from the front or the back
- Your arms should be at 90 degree angles and swing back and forth without crossing in front of your chest
- Your chest should be out forward, opening up your lungs to allow for easier breathing

When it comes to breathing, this is the new runner's biggest complaint. It feels out of control and they feel they have to stop. As I mentioned above, if this is the case, you need to slow down. Just slow down. When you have your 5k finished we can work on pace and speeding up, for now it is good enough to finish a 5k, even if it takes 40 minutes to complete. That said, in order to help your breathing while running, there are a few things that we can work on.

- Breathe through your mouth and your nose. This allows you to get as much oxygen as possible as quickly as possible. Simple to do. You never see a runner running at effort with their mouth closed.
- Use a breathing pattern like three strides per breath in and two strides per breath out. This means that each time your foot hits the ground you take a partial breath in or out. There are a number of advantages to using a breathing technique like this, but for one thing, it reduces the chances of getting a stitch.
- Counting your cadence when you run is really useful. Your cadence is the number of times your feet hit the ground while you are running. It is usually measured in strides per minute. Counting your cadence while using a breathing pattern, like the one above, takes your mind off the discomfort you may be experiencing. It also gives you a good idea of

your pace, much like a metronome would. It makes it much easier to know if you are going faster than normal.

I wish there was some magic button we could press to make this part of running easier, but there isn't. For now, just remember it's all about going slow, get to the finish of each session and before you know it, you'll have a 5k in the bag.

CHAPTER 6
DYNAMIC EXERCISES

THE DYNAMIC EXERCISES we will be doing will be used to get your relevant muscles warmed up and ready to work. We will be doing these after our initial brisk walk at the start of each session. A demonstration of these dynamic exercises can be viewed on Achieve Running Club Video Page

- Running in place
- High Knees
- Heel Flicks
- Straight Leg Kicks
- A - Skips
- High Skips
- Lunges
- Side Lunges
- Squats

. . .

We won't be doing all of these at every session, but as we go through the sessions we will be adding some more in. This shouldn't be too strenuous, but you may be out of breath when we finish these. Do your best and they will get easier the more you do them.

CHAPTER 7
POST WORKOUT STRETCHING

AFTER EACH WORKOUT, we will be doing some static stretching. When we exercise, our muscles tend to shorten and tense. The purpose of the static stretching will be to return your muscle to the length they were before your session. Each stretch should be held for 15 seconds to be most productive. A demonstration of each of these stretches can be viewed on my YouTube channel at Achieve Running Club.

- 3 x Stand tall, reach for the sky, on your toes and hold for 15 seconds
- Spread legs shoulder width apart, fingers interlocked bend at the hips, back level reach out in front - hold for 15 seconds
- Reach down intending to touch the ground - hold for 15 seconds

- Walk hands over to right ankle, put both hands around the right ankle - hold for 15 seconds
- Walk hands over to the left ankle, put both hands around the left ankle - hold for 15 seconds
- Slowly move back to the centre and slowly raise up
- Put left foot in front of the right, dig both heels into the ground, lean forward on a bent knee - hold for 15 seconds
- Put right foot in front of the left, dig both heels into the ground, lean forward on a bent knee - hold for 15 seconds
- Stand on left leg and hold the right foot in your hand bent at the knee, keep both knees together, push your hips forward - hold for 15 seconds
- Stand on right leg and hold the left foot in your hand bent at the knee, keep both knees together, push your hips forward - hold for 15 seconds
- Hold left arm straight out in front, bring it across your front, pull in with back of right hand - hold for 15 seconds
- Hold right arm straight out in front, bring it across your front, pull in with back of left hand - hold for 15 seconds

- Big circles with arms moving forwards - 15 seconds
- Big circles with arms moving backwards - 15 seconds

As with each part of your sessions, this portion of your workout is important and should never be skipped. It will go a long way to help prevent injuries and reduce lingering soreness.

CHAPTER 8
NUTRITION, HYDRATION & SLEEP

THIS IS a common subject that comes up when starting out with new runners. What do I eat before a run? How soon can I run after I eat? How much water should I drink? Only you will be able to answer these and only after some practice. Generally speaking, it is safe to say that your body should have enough energy stored to run a 5k without consuming a meal beforehand. However, you may find it easier with a light snack about two hours before you run. Something that is not going to upset your stomach and that is fairly quick to digest. Fruit or white carbohydrates of some sort would be ideal as these are digested quickly. If you wish to eat earlier than that, say three hours before running, you can probably eat more complex carbohydrates. But you will need to test your body to see what works best for you.

As for water, it is best practice to be fairly well

hydrated all day. As a minimum, one litre of water per day should be consumed. If you are running in a warm climate, then you should be drinking more. Always bring water with you when you are training so that you can drink at least 500ml after each session.

After a training session you should aim to get a meal including a good mix of protein, carbohydrates and fats. Too many people neglect to get enough protein in their diet. When you are involved in an exercise program it is so important to consume protein. This is what your body uses to build the muscle fibres back after the challenges you are giving them during your workout.

Taking up a new sport is exciting, but it is also a great opportunity to make positive changes to your lifestyle. This is a terrific opportunity to address any sleep issues you may have. Running is such a great sport to help anyone get their sleep regime on track. Your body will make much better gains from the exercise you perform if you give it ample rest and time to build back your muscles. Running promotes a healthy sleep cycle, so do your best to take advantage of the effort you are putting in.

CHAPTER 9
HOW SHOULD IT FEEL

YOU WILL HAVE good days and bad days. Every single runner on the planet will tell you that. Some days it feels easy and other days it feels hard. Don't be discouraged when you have a bad session. Give yourself a pat on the back for doing your best and getting through it. Tell yourself that the next one will be better, because it most likely will.

You should be running at what is known as conversation pace. This means you should be able to talk, maybe not comfortably, but you should be able to get some words out without gasping for breath. If this is too difficult, you need to slow down. For some new runners, this may feel like walking, but this is OK. The more often you get out and do these sessions, the more it will feel like running and less like walking.

WHAT TO DO IF YOU EXPERIENCE PAIN

As runners, we all experience soreness. This is normal, especially if you are new to the sport. You are using muscles and moving in ways that many of you haven't used or done in a long time, if ever. This is where you must take extra time to stretch as per the program. If you have time, you should stretch as often as you can, not just immediately after your running sessions. If you can squeeze in 10 minutes in the morning, or before bed, that would go a long way to helping with the soreness.

It is not uncommon for new runners to experience knee pain, calf pain or sore glutes after a few weeks. Most of the time this can be remedied with straight forward stretching. Sometimes this isn't enough, and you may want to have a foam roller at the ready. Just like stretching, foam-rolling can be done daily and will also be a substantial help. This is the case even if you aren't experiencing soreness or pain. If you can fit in a regular foam rolling session, you may be able to prevent the discomfort in the first place.

If, however, you are experiencing any sharp pains, it may be best to see a sports massage therapist or physiotherapist to see if they can offer some assistance. Most of the time, and I do mean most of the time, the pain is temporary and by continuing to run, stretch and foam roll your body will adapt and get used to this new exercise. The point is to not panic if you are experiencing these things.

You can see some examples of foam rolling on my youtube channel, Achieve Running Club.

CHAPTER 10
6 WEEK PROGRAM

THIS SIX WEEK program is designed to get you from not running all up to running the full 5k distance. You will have three sessions per week and will be asked to work on a specific coaching point during each week. Pay close attention to these coaching points as these will make running feel easier, particularly when you start running for a longer period of time. This plan has been paced out to ensure that anyone can go from the couch to completing the 5k.

There is an eight week plan further along in this book to cater for those people who can dedicate only two days per week.

CHAPTER 11
WEEK 1

SESSION 1 (DAY 1)

OK, you've chosen the 6-week program, good for you. Please don't skip ahead in the plan even if it feels easy to begin with. This plan has been proven to work over and over again for those who have a good starting point, so let's give this a good chance at working at its own pace. 6-weeks isn't too much to ask when it comes to building lifelong benefits. Let's go!

COACHING POINT

This week the coaching point we will be working on is posture. If you ever watch people running, you will see that many people when they are tired will have their shoulders tensed up near their ears. They will look tense all over, with their arms swinging across their body. It's natural to lose good form when you are tired, but that is when you really need it most.

Make a point to check in at regular intervals on your run and take a check on your posture. Maybe it is every time you pass a certain point on the track, or when you pass a certain tree, house, or telephone pole, it doesn't matter. Just take a mental check if you are running upright, chest out, shoulders relaxed and positioned back and down. Are you spilling the water from the bowl between your hips? Hopefully, the answer is no. Good running form can make you run much more efficiently, covering more ground in less time, with less effort. Keep working on your form every session.

Warm-up
Brisk walk warm-up - 5 minutes

Dynamic Warm-up

- Running in place - 20 seconds
- High Knees - 20 seconds
- Running in place - 20 seconds
- Heel flicks - 20 seconds
- Running in place - 20 seconds
- Straight Leg Kicks - 20 seconds

- Running in place - 20 seconds
- A - Skips - 20 seconds
- Running in place - 20 seconds
- Lunges - 10 (5 each leg)
- Running in place - 20 seconds

<u>Main Session</u>
5 reps of 30 seconds running followed by 90 seconds walking

———

After the 5th rep of 30 seconds running walk for 2 minutes

———

5 reps of 60 **seconds** running followed by 90 seconds walking

As this is the first session, I'll list it out to remove any confusion.

- run - 30 seconds
- Walk - 90 seconds

- run - 30 seconds
- Walk - 90 seconds
- run - 30 seconds
- Walk - 90 seconds
- run - 30 seconds
- Walk - 90 seconds
- run - 30 seconds
- **Walk - 2 minutes - this separates the two sets**
- run - 60 seconds
- Walk - 90 seconds
- run - 60 seconds
- Walk - 90 seconds
- run - 60 seconds
- Walk - 90 seconds
- run - 60 seconds
- Walk - 90 seconds
- run - 60 seconds

Cool-Down
Brisk walk cool-down - 5 minutes

Stretching Routine
As described in the Post Workout Stretching

SESSION 2 (DAY 2)

Warm-up

Brisk walk warm-up - 5 minutes

Dynamic Warm-up

- Running in place - 20 seconds
- High Knees - 20 seconds
- Running in place - 20 seconds
- Heel flicks - 20 seconds
- Running in place - 20 seconds
- Straight Leg Kicks - 20 seconds
- Running in place - 20 seconds
- A - Skips - 20 seconds
- Running in place - 20 seconds
- Lunges - 10 (5 each leg)
- Running in place - 20 seconds

Main Session

5 reps of 60 seconds running followed by 90 seconds walking

———

After the 5th rep of 30 seconds running walk for 2 minutes

———

5 reps of 60 seconds running followed by 90 seconds walking

Cool-Down
Brisk walk cool-down - 5 minutes

Stretching Routine
As described in the Post Workout Stretching

SESSION 3 (DAY 3)

Warm-up
Brisk walk warm-up - 5 minutes

Dynamic Warm-up

- Running in place - 20 seconds
- High Knees - 20 seconds
- Running in place - 20 seconds
- Heel flicks - 20 seconds
- Running in place - 20 seconds
- Straight Leg Kicks - 20 seconds
- Running in place - 20 seconds
- A - Skips - 20 seconds
- Running in place - 20 seconds
- Lunges - 10 (5 each leg)
- Running in place - 20 seconds

Main Session
5 reps of 60 seconds running followed by 60 seconds walking

After the 5th rep of 60 seconds running walk for 2 minutes

---

5 reps of 90 seconds running followed by 60 seconds walking

Cool-Down
Brisk walk cool-down - 5 minutes

Stretching Routine
As described in the Post Workout Stretching

CHAPTER 12
WEEK 2

COACHING POINT

You've been working on good running form over the course of the first 3 sessions. That's a great start, well done you! It should now feel almost natural to be running tall and efficiently. This next two weeks we will work on breathing techniques. This week, we will try to develop a good breathing rhythm. I suggest 2 strides per breath in, and 3 strides per breath out. This will help avoid stitches and is an excellent way to regulate your breathing as you go. It may be easiest to breathe this out loud, as I do in my instructional video here. At least until it becomes second nature while you are running.

SESSION 1 (DAY 4)

Warm-up
Brisk walk warm-up - 5 minutes

Dynamic Warm-up

- Running in place - 20 seconds
- High Knees - 20 seconds
- Running in place - 20 seconds
- Heel flicks - 20 seconds
- Running in place - 20 seconds
- Straight Leg Kicks - 20 seconds
- Running in place - 20 seconds
- A - Skips - 20 seconds
- Running in place - 20 seconds
- Lunges - 10 (5 each leg)
- Running in place - 20 seconds

Main Session
5 reps of 90 seconds running followed by 60 seconds walking

———

After the 5th rep of 60 seconds running walk for 2 minutes

5 reps of 90 seconds running followed by 60 seconds walking

Cool-Down
Brisk walk cool-down - 5 minutes

Stretching Routine
As described in the Post Workout Stretching

SESSION 2 (DAY 5)

Warm-up
Brisk walk warm-up - 5 minutes

Dynamic Warm-up

- Running in place - 20 seconds
- High Knees - 20 seconds
- Running in place - 20 seconds
- Heel flicks - 20 seconds
- Running in place - 20 seconds
- Straight Leg Kicks - 20 seconds
- Running in place - 20 seconds
- A - Skips - 20 seconds
- Running in place - 20 seconds

- Lunges - 10 (5 each leg)
- Running in place - 20 seconds

Main Session

5 reps of 60 seconds running followed by 60 seconds walking

After the 5th rep of 60 seconds running walk for 2 minutes

---

5 rep of 90 seconds running followed by 60 seconds walking

Cool-Down
Brisk walk cool-down - 5 minutes

Stretching Routine
As described in the Post Workout Stretching

SESSION 3 (DAY 6)

<u>Warm-up</u>

Brisk walk warm-up - 5 minutes

<u>Dynamic Warm-up</u>

- Running in place - 20 seconds
- High Knees - 20 seconds
- Running in place - 20 seconds
- Heel flicks - 20 seconds
- Running in place - 20 seconds
- Straight Leg Kicks - 20 seconds
- Running in place - 20 seconds
- A - Skips - 20 seconds
- Running in place - 20 seconds
- Lunges - 10 (5 each leg)
- Running in place - 20 seconds

<u>Main Session</u>
5 reps of 2 minutes running followed by 60 seconds walking

―――――

After the 5th rep of 2 minutes running walk for 2 minutes

5 reps of 2 minutes running followed by 60 seconds walking

Cool-Down
Brisk walk cool-down - 5 minutes

Stretching Routine
As described in the Post Workout Stretching

CHAPTER 13
WEEK 3

<u>COACHING POINT</u>

So you have some breathing techniques that will hopefully be working for you. It's a good time to remind you that if you are struggling to breathe, you are going too fast and need to slow down. You can work on going faster after we finish the first 5k. I have a 5k improvement book out that you can use to pick up the pace, but for now, let's focus on finishing. This week, we are going to continue working on these breathing techniques. Last week, the focus was on breathing rhythm. This week, we are going to count our cadence. You don't need to worry about how many strides per minute you are doing, that is something to deal with way down the road. Right now, it's about getting the cadence in your head in order to keep track of what your pace should be when running comfortably.

What you will be doing to track your cadence is every time your right (or left) foot hits the ground count 1, and continue up to 10, and then start at 1 once again.

1, 2, 3, 4, 5, 6, 7, 8, 9, 10,

1, 2, 3, 4, 5, 6, 7, 8, 9, 10…

This will give you a really good indication of when you are going too fast. This will also help occupy your brain while you are taking on these longer sessions. Any distraction is a good distraction.

This is a good time to also remind you that you are doing great. You've reached the hardest part of this whole program. When you get through these next two weeks, you have cracked it! Keep going.

SESSION 1 (DAY 7)

<u>Warm-up</u>
Brisk walk warm-up - 5 minutes

<u>Dynamic Warm-up</u>

- Running in place - 20 seconds
- High Knees - 20 seconds
- Running in place - 20 seconds
- Heel flicks - 20 seconds
- Running in place - 20 seconds
- Straight Leg Kicks - 20 seconds

- Running in place - 20 seconds
- A - Skips - 20 seconds
- Running in place - 20 seconds
- Lunges - 10 (5 each leg)
- Running in place - 20 seconds
- Side Lunges - 10 (5 each side)

Main Session

3 reps of 3 minutes running followed by 2 minutes walking

After the 3rd rep of 3 minutes running walk for 3 minutes

---

1 rep of 4 minutes running

Cool-Down

Brisk walk cool-down - 5 minutes

Stretching Routine

As described in the Post Workout Stretching

SESSION 2 (DAY 8)

<u>Warm-up</u>
Brisk walk warm-up - 5 minutes

<u>Dynamic Warm-up</u>

- Running in place - 20 seconds
- High Knees - 20 seconds
- Running in place - 20 seconds
- Heel flicks - 20 seconds
- Running in place - 20 seconds
- Straight Leg Kicks - 20 seconds
- Running in place - 20 seconds
- A - Skips - 20 seconds
- Running in place - 20 seconds
- Lunges - 10 (5 each leg)
- Running in place - 20 seconds
- Side Lunges - 10 (5 each side)

<u>Main Session</u>

3 reps of 4 minutes running followed by 60 seconds walking

After the 5th rep of 2 minutes running walk for 2 minutes

---

1 rep of 6 minutes running followed by 60 seconds walking

Cool-Down
Brisk walk cool-down - 5 minutes

Stretching Routine
As described in the Post Workout Stretching

SESSION 3 (DAY 9)

Warm-up
Brisk walk warm-up - 5 minutes

Dynamic Warm-up

- Running in place - 20 seconds
- High Knees - 20 seconds
- Running in place - 20 seconds
- Heel flicks - 20 seconds
- Running in place - 20 seconds
- Straight Leg Kicks - 20 seconds
- Running in place - 20 seconds

- A - Skips - 20 seconds
- Running in place - 20 seconds
- Lunges - 10 (5 each leg)
- Running in place - 20 seconds
- Side Lunges - 10 (5 each side)

Main Session

4 reps of 6 minutes running followed by 60 seconds walking recovery

Cool-Down

Brisk walk cool-down - 5 minutes

Stretching Routine

As described in the Post Workout Stretching

CHAPTER 14
WEEK 4

COACHING POINT

Week 4 already! Excellent work, you should be proud of yourself at getting beyond the halfway point. Let's keep up the momentum by continuing to work on your breathing. This week, let's go back to your breathing rhythm. This time, we are going to work on 2 strides breathing in and 3 strides breathing out. By alternating the last footfall on the last out breath you do a few different things. The first thing is that it can help prevent a cramp.

If you do develop a cramp, a method to help alleviate it more quickly is to change your breathing rhythm to always have your last out breath on the foot on the opposing side to the pain. This would require a change to the rhythm to a 2 strides per breath in and two strides per breath out. See an instructional video for a demonstration here: Achieve Running Club Videos.

SESSION 1 (DAY 10)

Warm-up
Brisk walk warm-up - 5 minutes

Dynamic Warm-up

- Running in place - 20 seconds
- High Knees - 20 seconds
- Running in place - 20 seconds
- Heel flicks - 20 seconds
- Running in place - 20 seconds
- Straight Leg Kicks - 20 seconds
- Running in place - 20 seconds
- A - Skips - 20 seconds
- Running in place - 20 seconds
- Lunges - 10 (5 each leg)
- Running in place - 20 seconds
- Side Lunges - 10 (5 each side)
- Running in place - 20 seconds
- Squats - 10

Main Session

4 reps of 6 minutes running followed by 60 seconds walking recovery

Cool-Down
=========

Brisk walk cool-down - 5 minutes

Stretching Routine
==================

As described in the Post Workout Stretching

SESSION 2 (DAY 11)

Warm-up
=======

Brisk walk warm-up - 5 minutes

Dynamic Warm-up
===============

- Running in place - 20 seconds
- High Knees - 20 seconds
- Running in place - 20 seconds
- Heel flicks - 20 seconds
- Running in place - 20 seconds
- Straight Leg Kicks - 20 seconds
- Running in place - 20 seconds
- A - Skips - 20 seconds
- Running in place - 20 seconds
- Lunges - 10 (5 each leg)
- Running in place - 20 seconds

- Side Lunges - 10 (5 each side)
- Running in place - 20 seconds
- Squats - 10

Main Session

2 reps of 10 minutes running with by 2 minutes walking recovery

Cool-Down

Brisk walk cool-down - 5 minutes

Stretching Routine

As described in the Post Workout Stretching

SESSION 3 (DAY 12)

Warm-up

Brisk walk warm-up - 5 minutes

Dynamic Warm-up

- Running in place - 20 seconds
- High Knees - 20 seconds
- Running in place - 20 seconds
- Heel flicks - 20 seconds
- Running in place - 20 seconds
- Straight Leg Kicks - 20 seconds

- Running in place - 20 seconds
- A - Skips - 20 seconds
- Running in place - 20 seconds
- Lunges - 10 (5 each leg)
- Running in place - 20 seconds
- Side Lunges - 10 (5 each side)
- Running in place 20 seconds
- Squats - 10

Main Session
2 reps of 10 minutes running with by 2 minutes walking recovery

Cool-Down
Brisk walk cool-down - 5 minutes

Stretching Routine
As described in the Post Workout Stretching

CHAPTER 15
WEEK 5

<u>COACHING POINT</u>

Fantastic! We are at week 5 and only 1 week to go before your first 5k. Starting this week, we will be putting it all together. Take regular mental checks on your form.

- You are upright with chest out
- Shoulders relaxed and down
- You are running tall
- You are using your arms to drive you forward and especially up the hills if there are any

You are using a breathing technique either:

- Counting to a rhythm
- Counting your cadence

SESSION 1 (DAY 13)

Warm-up
Brisk walk warm-up - 5 minutes

Dynamic Warm-up

- Running in place - 20 seconds
- High Knees - 20 seconds
- Running in place - 20 seconds
- Heel flicks - 20 seconds
- Running in place - 20 seconds
- Straight Leg Kicks - 20 seconds
- Running in place - 20 seconds
- A - Skips - 20 seconds
- Running in place - 20 seconds
- Lunges - 10 (5 each leg)
- Running in place - 20 seconds
- Side Lunges - 10 (5 each side)
- Running in place - 20 seconds
- Squats - 10

Main Session
1 rep of 20 minutes running

Cool-Down
Brisk walk cool-down - 5 minutes

Stretching Routine

As described in the Post Workout Stretching

SESSION 2 (DAY 14)

Warm-up

Brisk walk warm-up - 5 minutes

Dynamic Warm-up

- Running in place - 20 seconds
- High Knees - 20 seconds
- Running in place - 20 seconds
- Heel flicks - 20 seconds
- Running in place - 20 seconds
- Straight Leg Kicks - 20 seconds
- Running in place - 20 seconds
- A - Skips - 20 seconds
- Running in place - 20 seconds
- Lunges - 10 (5 each leg)
- Running in place - 20 seconds
- Side Lunges - 10 (5 each side)
- Running in place - 20 seconds
- Squats - 10

Main Session

1 rep of 25 minutes running

Cool-Down

Brisk walk cool-down - 5 minutes

Stretching Routine

As described in the Post Workout Stretching

SESSION 3 (DAY 15)

Warm-up

Brisk walk warm-up - 5 minutes

Dynamic Warm-up

- Running in place - 20 seconds
- High Knees - 20 seconds
- Running in place - 20 seconds
- Heel flicks - 20 seconds
- Running in place - 20 seconds
- Straight Leg Kicks - 20 seconds
- Running in place - 20 seconds
- A - Skips - 20 seconds
- Running in place - 20 seconds
- Lunges - 10 (5 each leg)
- Running in place - 20 seconds
- Side Lunges - 10 (5 each side)
- Running in place 20 seconds
- Squats - 10

Main Session
1 rep of 25 minutes running

Cool-Down
Brisk walk cool-down - 5 minutes

Stretching Routine
As described in the Post Workout Stretching

CHAPTER 16
WEEK 6

<u>COACHING POINT</u>

Great work getting to week 6! You are through the hardest part now and you should be feeling a little more confident in your abilities. During week 6 we will go back to working on form. For the next couple of weeks we will work on your arms. Your arms should be bent at the elbow at a 90 degree angle. They should be driving straight forward and backward. The idea is to not cross over in front of your chest as you run as this closes the chest up and makes it just that little bit harder to breathe. A good visual to keep in mind is to try to use your arms as if you are cross-country skiing and pushing yourself forward as your arm goes back. Another visual you may want to use is to drive your arm back as if you are trying to elbow someone directly behind you (we all want to do that now and again).

As your arms go, so your legs go. If you want to move your legs at a certain pace, you can begin by driving your arms at that pace. It is very difficult to move your arms and legs at a different speed. Try running at a slow pace and move your arms at a fast pace. See, very difficult. So, this week, let's work on that arm drive.

While you work on your arm drive, don't forget your good running form, your breathing and cadence techniques. Put it all together now and at the end of this week, you will have your first 5k done!

SESSION 1 (DAY 16)

<u>Warm-up</u>
Brisk walk warm-up - 5 minutes

<u>Dynamic Warm-up</u>

- Running in place - 20 seconds
- High Knees - 20 seconds
- Running in place - 20 seconds
- Heel flicks - 20 seconds
- Running in place - 20 seconds
- Straight Leg Kicks - 20 seconds
- Running in place - 20 seconds
- A - Skips - 20 seconds
- Running in place - 20 seconds

- Lunges - 10 (5 each leg)
- Running in place - 20 seconds
- Side Lunges - 10 (5 each side)
- Running in place - 20 seconds
- Squats - 10

Main Session
1 rep of 30 minutes running

Cool-Down
Brisk walk cool-down - 5 minutes

Stretching Routine
As described in the Post Workout Stretching

SESSION 2 (DAY 17)

Warm-up
Brisk walk warm-up - 5 minutes

Dynamic Warm-up

- Running in place - 20 seconds
- High Knees - 20 seconds
- Running in place - 20 seconds
- Heel flicks - 20 seconds

- Running in place - 20 seconds
- Straight Leg Kicks - 20 seconds
- Running in place - 20 seconds
- A - Skips - 20 seconds
- Running in place - 20 seconds
- Lunges - 10 (5 each leg)
- Running in place - 20 seconds
- Side Lunges - 10 (5 each side)
- Running in place - 20 seconds
- Squats - 10

Main Session

1 rep of 30 minutes running

Cool-Down

Brisk walk cool-down - 5 minutes

Stretching Routine

As described in the Post Workout Stretching

5K DAY (DAY 18)

Here you are! Finally, this is the day. Trust all the work you've put in. Trust your training. Trust the program. Go out and run your 5k. Take pride in the fact that you are about to complete the 5k distance. By all means, please give me your feedback here: Achieve Running Club 5k Plan Feedback

Warm-up
Brisk walk warm-up - 5 minutes

Dynamic Warm-up

- Running in place - 20 seconds
- High Knees - 20 seconds
- Running in place - 20 seconds
- Heel flicks - 20 seconds
- Running in place - 20 seconds
- Straight Leg Kicks - 20 seconds
- Running in place - 20 seconds
- A - Skips - 20 seconds
- Running in place - 20 seconds
- Lunges - 10 (5 each leg)
- Running in place - 20 seconds
- Side Lunges - 10 (5 each side)
- Running in place 20 seconds
- Squats - 10

Main Session
Run Your 5k

Cool-Down
Brisk walk cool-down - 5 minutes

Stretching Routine
As described in the Post Workout Stretching

CHAPTER 17
8 WEEK PROGRAM

THIS 8 WEEK program is designed to get you from not running all up to running the full 5k distance. You will have two sessions per week and will be asked to work on a specific coaching point during each week. Pay close attention to these coaching points as these will make running feel easier, particularly when you start running for a longer period of time. This plan has been paced out to ensure that anyone can go from the couch to completing the 5k.

CHAPTER 18
WEEK 1

SESSION 1 (DAY 1)

YOU HAVE your gear including a watch to know when to start and stop, possibly a running partner or two, and a place to do your session. That's all you need. Here we go!

COACHING POINT

This week the coaching point we will be working on is posture. If you ever watch people running, you will see that many people when they are tired will have their shoulders tensed up near their ears. They will look tense all over, with their arms swinging across their body. It's natural to lose good form when you are tired, but that is when you really need good form.

Make a point to check in at regular intervals and take a check on your posture. Maybe it is every time you pass a certain point on the track, or when you pass a certain tree, house, or telephone pole, it doesn't matter. Just take a mental check if you are running upright, chest out, shoulders relaxed and positioned back and down. Are you spilling the water from the bowl between your hips? Hopefully, the answer is no. Good running form can make you run much more efficiently, covering more ground in less time, with less effort. Keep working on your form every session.

Warm-up
Brisk walk warm-up - 5 minutes

Dynamic Warm-up

- Running in place - 20 seconds
- High Knees - 20 seconds
- Running in place - 20 seconds
- Heel flicks - 20 seconds
- Running in place - 20 seconds
- Straight Leg Kicks - 20 seconds
- Running in place - 20 seconds
- A - Skips - 20 seconds
- Running in place - 20 seconds
- Lunges - 10 (5 each leg)

- Running in place - 20 seconds

<u>Main Session</u>
5 reps of 30 seconds running followed by 90 seconds walking

———

After the 5th rep of 30 seconds running walk for 2 minutes

———

5 reps of 30 seconds running followed by 90 seconds walking

As this is the first one, I'll list it out to remove any confusion.

Set 1:

- run - 30 seconds
- Walk - 90 seconds
- run - 30 seconds
- Walk - 90 seconds
- run - 30 seconds

- Walk - 90 seconds
- run - 30 seconds
- Walk - 90 seconds
- run - 30 seconds

End of set 1 - Recovery

- Walk - 2 minutes - this separates the two sets (make sure you are breathing deeply and getting the most benefit of your recovery)

Set 2:

- run - 30 seconds
- Walk - 90 seconds
- run - 30 seconds
- Walk - 90 seconds
- run - 30 seconds
- Walk - 90 seconds
- run - 30 seconds
- Walk - 90 seconds
- run - 30 seconds

End of main session

Cool-Down
Brisk walk cool-down - 5 minutes

Stretching Routine
As described in the Post Workout Stretching

SESSION 2 (DAY 2)

Warm-up
Brisk walk warm-up - 5 minutes

Dynamic Warm-up

- Running in place - 20 seconds
- High Knees - 20 seconds
- Running in place - 20 seconds
- Heel flicks - 20 seconds
- Running in place - 20 seconds
- Straight Leg Kicks - 20 seconds
- Running in place - 20 seconds
- A - Skips - 20 seconds
- Running in place - 20 seconds
- Lunges - 10 (5 each leg)
- Running in place - 20 seconds

Main Session
5 reps of 30 seconds running followed by 90 seconds walking

After the 5th rep of 30 seconds running walk for 2 minutes

---

5 reps of 60 seconds running followed by 90 seconds walking (note the longer rep)

Cool-Down
Brisk walk cool-down - 5 minutes

Stretching Routine
As described in the Post Workout Stretching

CHAPTER 19
WEEK 2

COACHING POINT

Good running form is such an important aspect to making running easier that we will continue to focus on this. It will help us achieve our goal of finishing the 5k distance. Once again, in your sessions during week 2, make a point to check in at regular intervals and take a check on your posture. Whatever you used as a queue to check in during week 1, use that again. Take a mental check that you are running upright, chest out, shoulders relaxed and positioned back and down. You shouldn't be so upright that you have a slight lean back, just run *tall*. Keep working on your form every session.

SESSION 1 (DAY 3)

<u>Warm-up</u>
Brisk walk warm-up - 5 minutes

<u>Dynamic Warm-up</u>

- Running in place - 20 seconds
- High Knees - 20 seconds
- Running in place - 20 seconds
- Heel flicks - 20 seconds
- Running in place - 20 seconds
- Straight Leg Kicks - 20 seconds
- Running in place - 20 seconds
- A - Skips - 20 seconds
- Running in place - 20 seconds
- Lunges - 10 (5 each leg)
- Running in place - 20 seconds

<u>Main Session</u>

5 reps of 60 seconds running followed by 60 seconds walking

After the 5th rep of 60 seconds running walk for 2

minutes

---

5 reps of 90 seconds running followed by 60 seconds walking

Cool-Down
Brisk walk cool-down - 5 minutes

Stretching Routine
As described in the Post Workout Stretching

SESSION 2 (DAY 4)

Warm-up
Brisk walk warm-up - 5 minutes

Dynamic Warm-up

- Running in place - 20 seconds
- High Knees - 20 seconds
- Running in place - 20 seconds
- Heel flicks - 20 seconds
- Running in place - 20 seconds
- Straight Leg Kicks - 20 seconds
- Running in place - 20 seconds

- A - Skips - 20 seconds
- Running in place - 20 seconds
- Lunges - 10 (5 each leg)
- Running in place - 20 seconds

Main Session

5 reps of 60 seconds running followed by 60 seconds walking

After the 5th rep of 60 seconds running walk for 2 minutes

---

5 rep of 90 seconds running followed by 60 seconds walking

Cool-Down
Brisk walk cool-down - 5 minutes

Stretching Routine
As described in the Post Workout Stretching

CHAPTER 20
WEEK 3

COACHING POINT

You've been working on good running form over the course of the first 6 sessions. That's a great start, well done you! It should now feel almost natural to be running tall and efficiently. This next two weeks we will work on breathing techniques. This week, we will try to develop a good breathing rhythm. I suggest 2 strides per breath in, and 3 strides per breath out. This will help avoid stitches and is an excellent way to regulate your breathing as you go. It may be easiest to breathe this out loud, as I do in my instructional video here. At least until it becomes second nature while you are running.

SESSION 1 (DAY 5)

Warm-up

Brisk walk warm-up - 5 minutes

Dynamic Warm-up

- Running in place - 20 seconds
- High Knees - 20 seconds
- Running in place - 20 seconds
- Heel flicks - 20 seconds
- Running in place - 20 seconds
- Straight Leg Kicks - 20 seconds
- Running in place - 20 seconds
- A - Skips - 20 seconds
- Running in place - 20 seconds
- Lunges - 10 (5 each leg)
- Running in place - 20 seconds
- Side Lunges - 10 (5 each side)

Main Session

5 reps of 2 minutes running followed by 60 seconds walking

———

After the 5th rep of 2 minutes running walk for 2 minutes

———

5 reps of 2 minutes running followed by 60 seconds walking

Cool-Down
Brisk walk cool-down - 5 minutes

Stretching Routine
As described in the Post Workout Stretching

SESSION 2 (DAY 6)

Warm-up
Brisk walk warm-up - 5 minutes

Dynamic Warm-up

- Running in place - 20 seconds
- High Knees - 20 seconds
- Running in place - 20 seconds
- Heel flicks - 20 seconds
- Running in place - 20 seconds
- Straight Leg Kicks - 20 seconds
- Running in place - 20 seconds
- A - Skips - 20 seconds
- Running in place - 20 seconds
- Lunges - 10 (5 each leg)
- Running in place - 20 seconds

- Side Lunges - 10 (5 each side)

Main Session

3 reps of 3 minutes running followed by 2 minutes walking

———

After the 3rd rep of 3 minutes running walk for 3 minutes

———

1 rep of 4 minutes running

Cool-Down
Brisk walk cool-down - 5 minutes

Stretching Routine
As described in the Post Workout Stretching

CHAPTER 21
WEEK 4

COACHING POINT

So you have some breathing techniques that will hopefully be working for you. It's a good time to remind you that if you are struggling to breathe, you are going too fast and need to slow down. You can work on going faster after we finish the first 5k. I have a 5k improvement book out that you can use to pick up the pace, but for now, let's focus on finishing. This week, we are going to continue working on these breathing techniques. Last week, the focus was on breathing rhythm. This week, we are going to count our cadence. You don't need to worry about how many strides per minute you are doing, that is something to deal with way down the road. Right now, it's about getting the cadence in your head in order to keep track of what your pace should be when running comfortably.

What you will be doing to track your cadence is every time your right (or left) foot hits the ground count 1, and continue up to 10, and then start at 1 once again.

1, 2, 3, 4, 5, 6, 7, 8, 9, 10,

1, 2, 3, 4, 5, 6, 7, 8, 9, 10…

This will give you a really good indication of when you are going too fast. This will also help occupy your brain while you are taking on these longer sessions. Any distraction is a good distraction.

This is a good time to also remind you that you are doing great. You've reached the hardest part of this whole program. When you get through these next two weeks, you have cracked it! Keep going.

SESSION 1 (DAY 7)

Warm-up
Brisk walk warm-up - 5 minutes

Dynamic Warm-up

- Running in place - 20 seconds
- High Knees - 20 seconds
- Running in place - 20 seconds
- Heel flicks - 20 seconds
- Running in place - 20 seconds

- Straight Leg Kicks - 20 seconds
- Running in place - 20 seconds
- A - Skips - 20 seconds
- Running in place - 20 seconds
- Lunges - 10 (5 each leg)
- Running in place - 20 seconds
- Side Lunges - 10 (5 each side)
- Running in place - 20 seconds
- Squats - 10

Main Session
3 reps of 3 minutes running followed by 60 seconds walking

———

After the 3rd rep of 3 minutes running walk for 3 minutes

———

1 rep of 4 minutes running followed by 60 seconds walking

Cool-Down
Brisk walk cool-down - 5 minutes

Stretching Routine
As described in the Post Workout Stretching

SESSION 2 (DAY 8)

Warm-up
Brisk walk warm-up - 5 minutes

Dynamic Warm-up

- Running in place - 20 seconds
- High Knees - 20 seconds
- Running in place - 20 seconds
- Heel flicks - 20 seconds
- Running in place - 20 seconds
- Straight Leg Kicks - 20 seconds
- Running in place - 20 seconds
- A - Skips - 20 seconds
- Running in place - 20 seconds
- Lunges - 10 (5 each leg)
- Running in place - 20 seconds
- Side Lunges - 10 (5 each side)
- Running in place - 20 seconds
- Squats - 10

Main Session

4 reps of 6 minutes running with by 90 seconds walking recovery

Cool-Down
Brisk walk cool-down - 5 minutes

Stretching Routine
As described in the Post Workout Stretching

CHAPTER 22
WEEK 5

COACHING POINT

Week 5 already! Excellent work, you should be proud of yourself for reaching the halfway point. Let's keep up the momentum by continuing to work on your breathing. This week, let's go back to your breathing rhythm. This time, we are going to work on 2 strides breathing in and 3 strides breathing out. By alternating the last footfall on the last out breath you do a few different things. The first thing is that it can help prevent a cramp.

If you do develop a cramp, a method to help alleviate it more quickly is to change your breathing rhythm to always have your last out breath on the foot on the opposing side. This would require a change to the rhythm to a 2 strides per breath in and two strides per breath out. See an instructional video for a demonstration here: Achieve Running Club Videos.

SESSION 1 (DAY 9)

Warm-up
Brisk walk warm-up - 5 minutes

Dynamic Warm-up

- Running in place - 20 seconds
- High Knees - 20 seconds
- Running in place - 20 seconds
- Heel flicks - 20 seconds
- Running in place - 20 seconds
- Straight Leg Kicks - 20 seconds
- Running in place - 20 seconds
- A - Skips - 20 seconds
- Running in place - 20 seconds
- Lunges - 10 (5 each leg)
- Running in place - 20 seconds
- Side Lunges - 10 (5 each side)
- Running in place - 20 seconds
- Squats - 10

Main Session
4 reps of 6 minutes running with by 60 seconds walking recovery

Cool-Down

Brisk walk cool-down - 5 minutes

Stretching Routine
As described in the Post Workout Stretching

SESSION 2 (DAY 10)

Warm-up
Brisk walk warm-up - 5 minutes

Dynamic Warm-up

- Running in place - 20 seconds
- High Knees - 20 seconds
- Running in place - 20 seconds
- Heel flicks - 20 seconds
- Running in place - 20 seconds
- Straight Leg Kicks - 20 seconds
- Running in place - 20 seconds
- A - Skips - 20 seconds
- Running in place - 20 seconds
- Lunges - 10 (5 each leg)
- Running in place - 20 seconds
- Side Lunges - 10 (5 each side)
- Running in place - 20 seconds
- Squats - 10

Main Session
2 reps of 10 minutes running with by 2 minutes walking recovery

Cool-Down
Brisk walk cool-down - 5 minutes

Stretching Routine
As described in the Post Workout Stretching

CHAPTER 23
WEEK 6

COACHING POINT

Great work getting to week 6! You are through the hardest part now and you should be feeling a little more confident in your abilities. During week 6 we will go back to working on form. For the next couple of weeks we will work on your arms. Your arms should be bent at the elbow at a 90 degree angle. They should be driving straight forward and backward. The idea is to not cross over in front of your chest as you run as this closes the chest up and makes it just that little bit harder to breathe. A good visual to keep in mind is to try to use your arms as if you are cross-country skiing and pushing yourself forward as your arm goes back. Another visual you may want to use is to drive your arm back as if you are trying to elbow someone directly behind you (we all want to do that now and again).

As your arms go, so your legs go. If you want to move your legs at a certain pace, you can begin by driving your arms at that pace. It is very difficult to move your arms and legs at a different speed. Try running at a slow pace and move your arms at a fast pace. See, very difficult. So, this week, let's work on that arm drive.

SESSION 1 (DAY 11)

<u>Warm-up</u>
Brisk walk warm-up - 5 minutes

<u>Dynamic Warm-up</u>

- Running in place - 20 seconds
- High Knees - 20 seconds
- Running in place - 20 seconds
- Heel flicks - 20 seconds
- Running in place - 20 seconds
- Straight Leg Kicks - 20 seconds
- Running in place - 20 seconds
- A - Skips - 20 seconds
- Running in place - 20 seconds
- Lunges - 10 (5 each leg)
- Running in place - 20 seconds
- Side Lunges - 10 (5 each side)
- Running in place - 20 seconds

- Squats - 10

Main Session
2 reps of 10 minutes running with by 2 minutes walking recovery

Cool-Down
Brisk walk cool-down - 5 minutes

Stretching Routine
As described in the Post Workout Stretching

SESSION 2 (DAY 12)

Warm-up
Brisk walk warm-up - 5 minutes

Dynamic Warm-up

- Running in place - 20 seconds
- High Knees - 20 seconds
- Running in place - 20 seconds
- Heel flicks - 20 seconds
- Running in place - 20 seconds
- Straight Leg Kicks - 20 seconds
- Running in place - 20 seconds
- A - Skips - 20 seconds

- Running in place - 20 seconds
- Lunges - 10 (5 each leg)
- Running in place - 20 seconds
- Side Lunges - 10 (5 each side)
- Running in place - 20 seconds
- Squats - 10

<u>Main Session</u>
1 rep of 20 minutes running

<u>Cool-Down</u>
Brisk walk cool-down - 5 minutes

<u>Stretching Routine</u>
As described in the Post Workout Stretching

CHAPTER 24
WEEK 7

COACHING POINT

Fantastic! We are at week 7 and only 2 weeks to go before your first 5k. Starting this week, we will be putting it all together. Take regular mental checks on your form.

- You are upright with chest out
- Shoulders relaxed and down
- You are running tall
- You are using your arms to drive you forward and especially up the hills if there are any

You are using a breathing technique either:

- Counting to a rhythm
- Counting your cadence

SESSION 1 (DAY 13)

Warm-up
Brisk walk warm-up - 5 minutes

Dynamic Warm-up

- Running in place - 20 seconds
- High Knees - 20 seconds
- Running in place - 20 seconds
- Heel flicks - 20 seconds
- Running in place - 20 seconds
- Straight Leg Kicks - 20 seconds
- Running in place - 20 seconds
- A - Skips - 20 seconds
- Running in place - 20 seconds
- Lunges - 10 (5 each leg)
- Running in place - 20 seconds
- Side Lunges - 10 (5 each side)
- Running in place - 20 seconds
- Squats - 10

Main Session
1 rep of 20 minutes running

Cool-Down
Brisk walk cool-down - 5 minutes

Stretching Routine

As described in the Post Workout Stretching

SESSION 2 (DAY 14)

Warm-up

Brisk walk warm-up - 5 minutes

Dynamic Warm-up

- Running in place - 20 seconds
- High Knees - 20 seconds
- Running in place - 20 seconds
- Heel flicks - 20 seconds
- Running in place - 20 seconds
- Straight Leg Kicks - 20 seconds
- Running in place - 20 seconds
- A - Skips - 20 seconds
- Running in place - 20 seconds
- Lunges - 10 (5 each leg)
- Running in place - 20 seconds
- Side Lunges - 10 (5 each side)
- Running in place - 20 seconds
- Squats - 10

Main Session

1 rep of 25 minutes running

Cool-Down
Brisk walk cool-down - 5 minutes

Stretching Routine
As described in the Post Workout Stretching

CHAPTER 25
WEEK 8

COACHING POINT

You have made it to the last week. Congratulations! The hardest of the work is done and you are about to finally be able to call yourself a runner. A proper runner. Well done. For coaching points, remind yourself that you are amazing. Remind yourself that you are about to accomplish something you never thought possible. Enjoy this week of training and most importantly, relish in the last session of the week, your target 5k.

SESSION 1 (DAY 15)

Warm-up

Brisk walk warm-up - 5 minutes

. . .

Dynamic Warm-up

- Running in place - 20 seconds
- High Knees - 20 seconds
- Running in place - 20 seconds
- Heel flicks - 20 seconds
- Running in place - 20 seconds
- Straight Leg Kicks - 20 seconds
- Running in place - 20 seconds
- A - Skips - 20 seconds
- Running in place - 20 seconds
- Lunges - 10 (5 each leg)
- Running in place - 20 seconds
- Side Lunges - 10 (5 each side)
- Running in place - 20 seconds
- Squats - 10

Main Session
1 rep of 30 minutes running

Cool-Down
Brisk walk cool-down - 5 minutes

Stretching Routine

As described in the Post Workout Stretching

5K DAY (DAY 16)

Here you are! Finally, this is the day. Trust all the work you've put in. Trust your training. Trust the program. Go out and run your 5k. Take pride in the fact that you are about to complete the 5k distance. By all means, please give me your feedback here: Achieve Running Club 5k Plan Feedback

Warm-up
Brisk walk warm-up - 5 minutes

Dynamic Warm-up

- Running in place - 20 seconds
- High Knees - 20 seconds
- Running in place - 20 seconds
- Heel flicks - 20 seconds
- Running in place - 20 seconds
- Straight Leg Kicks - 20 seconds
- Running in place - 20 seconds
- A - Skips - 20 seconds
- Running in place - 20 seconds
- Lunges - 10 (5 each leg)
- Running in place - 20 seconds

- Side Lunges - 10 (5 each side)
- Running in place 20 seconds
- Squats - 10

<u>Main Session</u>
Run Your 5k

<u>Cool-Down</u>
Brisk walk cool-down - 5 minutes

<u>Stretching Routine</u>
As described in the Post Workout Stretching

CHAPTER 26
WHAT'S NEXT

WHERE DO you go from here? For a great many of you, you will have made some running friends and now is the time to continue enjoying running your 5k's. Keep at it and remember consistency is king.

The next book in the Achieve More in Running series is Step Up to 10k. In this one you will get a 5k improvement plan as well as a plan to bring you up to the 10k distance. This book now available on Amazon.

For now, venture out and look for local parkruns. Scour Facebook and Google for local 5k's. You will be able to find some local runs just about every time of the year.

WHAT IS PARKRUN?

parkrun is a movement. It is a community of runners who get together every Saturday morning to run a free, timed 5k. There are parkruns all over the world so hopefully you have one near you.

For a great many of my Couch to 5k groups we've used the local parkrun as our graduating 5k run. It is well known as a supportive group with great encouragement from the volunteers. Because I've relied on parkrun for my groups I also volunteer regularly and I enjoy it every time. Everyone is encouraged to complete the Saturday morning route in any way they can.

parkrun is a wonderful place to watch the best of humanity come together. This is an event for everyone and you can witness firsthand the pride in all of the finishers when it has been completed. You know there is a community spirit at a parkrun because very few people finish the run and then take off straight away. Most runners stick around, congratulate other runners and discuss everything from that morning's run to the state of the course.

CONGRATULATIONS

YOU'VE DONE IT!

If you enjoyed this program, **please leave a positive review of this book on Amazon or wherever you purchased it**. It is so important to coaches and authors who are producing quality work for distribution.

It is a great way for this book to be put in front of more people. I've enjoyed working with you and please look for more of my books and training programs by browsing Running Books. You will find more advanced, easy to follow programs for hitting your future distance and speed goals. For now, bask in the greatness of what you just achieved. I am proud of you and you should be too!

Next up is Step Up to 10k book now available on Amazon. Browse them all on my <u>Amazon author page</u>.

WIN A FREE MONTH OF PERSONAL COACHING

How about getting some personal one-to-one coaching. I offer one free month of coaching to one reader of my books every single month. It's very easy to be in with a chance to win. Simply go to Amazon and post an honest review of this book. Then, in order to let me know it was you, click (or navigate to) https://jmruncoach.com/book-feedback and paste that same review along with your email address. That's it, you are in with a chance. I would love to work with you personally and see you hit your running goals.

ADDITIONAL RESOURCES

If you are interested in learning more about the author or need some additional inspiration, my memoir <u>A Heart for Running: How Running Saved My Life</u> is available on Amazon.

I would really like to hear from you with feedback. I am very much interested in your result from either your first 10k or from your target 5k race. Please reach out to me on one of the following links:

    Blog - https://AHeartForRunning.com
    Facebook - https://facebook.com/aheartforrunning
    Instagram - https://instagram.com/jmruncoach
    YouTube - https://youtube.com/@jmruncoach

ALSO BY JOHN MCDONNELL

A Heart for Running: How Running Saved My Life

In 2010, John McDonnell wasn't a runner; he was just an ordinary guy leading an ordinary life. Until one fateful day, when he stumbled upon vacation photos that revealed a stark truth – he had become overweight. Determined to reclaim his health and vitality, he embarked on a journey that would forever alter the course of his life: he started running.

What began as a quest to shed pounds quickly evolved into an unrelenting passion for running. John's transformation was nothing short of remarkable; he transitioned from 5K races to conquering 10K, half-marathons, and ultimately, the full marathon. Each step was fueled by an insatiable desire for self-improvement, and it became evident that running was his lifeline.

In 2017, adversity struck in the form of a devastating stroke, a dire consequence of an unsuspecting 11mm hole in his heart. For many, this setback might have marked the end of the road, but not for John. With unwavering determination and sheer grit, he embarked on a journey to reclaim his life once more.

"A Heart for Running" is more than just a running memoir; it's a testament to the incredible power of the human spirit. John's story is one of dedication, passion, and relentless perseverance. It's about defying the odds, refusing to succumb to setbacks, and emerging stronger on the other side.

Could John fulfill his dream of making a full comeback in the sport that had not only transformed his physique but also saved his life? Follow his emotional rollercoaster as he races against time and physical barriers, all in pursuit of the elusive 3-hour marathon barrier. His journey unfolds with raw honesty and humor, inviting you into his world of sweat, triumphs, and occasional misadventures.

Throughout "A Heart for Running," John invites you to share in his experiences, spanning over 30 marathons across Ireland, the UK, and beyond. From the exhilarating highs of crossing finish lines to the humbling lows of cramps and exhaustion, his storytelling paints a vivid picture of the runner's life.

Join John in this inspiring memoir, where the finish line is just the beginning of a new challenge, and where every step is a testament to the incredible potential within us all. "A Heart for Running" is not just a running book; it's a reminder that no obstacle is insurmountable, and that the journey is as extraordinary as the destination.

Experience the highs, lows, and the indomitable spirit of a man who refused to be defined by his setbacks. Discover the power of running to heal, transform, and ultimately transcend the limits of what's possible. John's journey is an inspiration to us all, proving that no matter your age, circumstances, or previous experience, the road ahead is yours to conquer.

What People Are Saying:

"**Plot/Idea:** McDonnell's perseverance is contagious. His honest approach to his process will inspire others to get off the couch and hit the pavement. While we often think of those that are ranked athletes as people who are physically gifted in some way, McDonnell proves that this is not the case with his compelling story and approach to his hard work.

Prose: McDonnell's compelling story is easy to read and highly inspirational. His encouraging personality shines through his writing.

Character/Execution: The level of detail McDonnell offers, notably, about his training schedule and techniques, proves to be a benefit for readers aspiring to challenge themselves physically." - The BookLife Prize

"An amazing read, relatable, thought provoking and lessons for us all to remember what is truly important!" - **Teresa McDaid - Athletics Ireland**

"A Heart for Running is an emotional rollercoaster, and you feel every single moment with John. Running quite literally saved his life and his story is an inspiration and a beacon of hope for us all." - **Irish Runner Magazine**

Running for Beginners: The Easiest Guide to Running Your First 5K In Only 6 Weeks

Unlock Your Inner Runner and Achieve the Impossible

Have you ever watched a marathon or a local 5k race and felt that deep-seated desire to join the ranks of those fleet-footed runners, to feel the exhilaration of crossing the finish line? You're not alone. Running has a unique allure, a primal call to push your limits, and discover what your body and mind are truly capable of. But where do you start? How do you go from being a non-runner to someone who can confidently run a 5k race without stopping? The answer lies within the pages of "Running for Beginners."

In this comprehensive and easy-to-follow guide, John, a seasoned runner and experienced coach, takes you on a transformative journey from complete novice to a confident 5k finisher in just 6 weeks. Whether you're an absolute beginner or someone who hasn't laced up running shoes in years, this book is your roadmap to success.

A Guided Journey to 5k Success

John understands the challenges that beginners face because he's been there himself. He knows the doubts, the fears, and the questions that can hold you back. That's why he's crafted this book to be your ultimate companion, offering guidance, motivation, and a step-by-step plan to turn your running aspirations into reality.

Inside "Running for Beginners," you'll discover:

Week-by-Week Training Plans: John has designed a 6-week training program that gradually builds your endurance and stamina. Each week, you'll receive clear instructions on when, where, and how far to run. The plan is tailored for beginners, ensuring that you progress at a pace that's comfortable for you.

Coaching Tips from an Expert: John's coaching expertise shines through in his advice on form, technique, and injury prevention. You'll learn how to run efficiently and avoid common mistakes that new runners often make.

The Basics You Need to Know: From choosing the right running shoes to understanding proper nutrition and hydration, "Running for Beginners" covers all the essential elements of becoming a successful runner.

Mental Toughness. Running is not just a physical endeavor; it's a mental one too. John shares strategies to help you stay motivated, overcome mental barriers, and develop the mental fortitude needed to complete your first 5k.

A Community of Runners: Join a community of like-minded individuals who are on their own running journeys. Connect with others, share your progress, and find the support you need to stay motivated and accountable.

Your Journey Starts Today

Imagine the feeling of accomplishment as you cross the finish line of your first 5k race. Picture the smiles, cheers, and sense of pride that await you. With "Running for Beginners" as your guide, that dream can become your reality. This book is not just about running; it's about discovering your true potential and proving to yourself that you can achieve anything you set your mind to.

Are you ready to take that first step, to put on your running shoes and embark on a journey that will change your life? The road to becoming a runner starts right here, right now. Join John and countless others who have transformed themselves through the power of running. It's time to lace up, hit the pavement, and make your first 5k race a reality.

Your First 5k Awaits.

Order your copy of "Running for Beginners: The Easiest Guide to Running Your First 5k in Only 6 Weeks" and begin your journey to becoming a confident and accomplished runner today.

Step Up to 10k: Improve Your 5k Time and Train for a 10k

Elevate Your Running Journey from 5K to 10K

Ready to transform your running prowess after conquering the 5K? "Step Up to 10K" is your comprehensive guide to becoming a 10K champion. Crafted by a seasoned running coach, this book unveils advanced training techniques and expert insights to help you reach new heights in your running endeavors.

As you embark on this exhilarating journey, you'll discover the keys to mastering both uphill and downhill terrains, thanks to our comprehensive coaching tips. Dive deep into the world of interval training, learn to harness the power of tempo runs, and embark on progressions that will propel your running prowess to new horizons.

Whether you're in your first or second year of training, this book is meticulously designed to ensure a seamless transition from 5K to 10K. But it doesn't stop there. Our specially designed training plan isn't just about conquering the 10K; it's about turbocharging your 5K performance as well, making this the year of personal records.

Your Guide to Running Excellence

"Step Up to 10K" is more than just a book; it's your portal to cutting-edge running expertise. Throughout these pages, you'll find access to exclusive video guides on essential topics like breathing techniques, dynamic drills, and post-run stretching – all aimed at optimizing your performance and preventing injuries.

Your running journey is about more than just races; it's about personal growth, resilience, and achieving feats you once thought impossible. This book is your trusted companion on this journey, offering guidance and motivation every step of the way.

Transform Your Running Experience

Transform your 10K journey into an immensely rewarding experience. With "Step Up to 10K" as your trusted companion, your running goals are well within reach. Whether you're conquering new distances or chasing personal bests, this guide has got you covered.

It's time to lace up your running shoes, set your sights on new horizons, and make this year one filled with remarkable achievements. Whether you're a novice or an experienced runner, "Step Up to 10K" will take your running to the next level.

Don't wait any longer. Elevate your running journey to new heights, and unlock your full running potential. Make this year the year you become a 10K champion.

"Step Up to 10K: Improve Your 5k Time and Train for a 10k" – your ultimate key to running greatness.

Running Your First Marathon Made EASY: All the Secrets You Need to Know for First Marathon Success

Running Your First Marathon Made EASY: All the Secrets You Need for First Marathon Success

Running Your First Marathon Made EASY is your indispensable companion on the exhilarating journey from apprehension to triumph as you prepare for and conquer your first marathon. Authored by seasoned coach John McDonnell, this comprehensive guide offers a roadmap for novice runners, providing invaluable insights and expert advice garnered from McDonnell's extensive experience both as a marathoner and as a coach who has mentored hundreds of first-time marathoners to success.

The journey of running a marathon is not merely a physical feat; it is a test of mental fortitude, perseverance, and self-belief. McDonnell begins by empathizing with the apprehension and doubts that often accompany the decision to undertake such a monumental challenge. From the initial incredulity of being persuaded to embark on this journey to the eventual euphoria of crossing the finish line, McDonnell assures readers that not only is it possible to complete a marathon, but it can also be an immensely rewarding and transformative experience.

Drawing on his own experiences and those of the athletes he has coached, McDonnell emphasizes that marathon running is as much about personal growth and development as it is about physical endurance. Through dedicated training, healthy lifestyle choices, and a positive mindset, runners can not only conquer the 26.2-mile distance but also emerge stronger, more confident, and capable of achieving their goals in various aspects of life.

The book outlines a comprehensive 20-week training plan, meticulously designed to guide readers through every stage of preparation, from the initial days of nervous anticipation to the grueling long runs and tapering period leading up to race day. McDonnell leaves no stone unturned, addressing crucial aspects such as nutrition, hydration, recovery, and mental resilience, ensuring that readers are well-equipped to tackle the challenges they will encounter along the way.

Furthermore, McDonnell shares invaluable lessons learned from his own marathon experiences and those of his proteges, offering practical tips and advice to help readers avoid common pitfalls and navigate the race day with confidence. From pacing strategies to gear recommendations, every aspect of the marathon journey is carefully considered to empower readers to achieve their personal best.

In addition to being a comprehensive training guide, "Running Your First Marathon Made EASY" serves as a source of inspiration and motivation for aspiring marathoners. McDonnell's unwavering belief in the attainability of this ambitious goal shines through, encouraging readers to embrace the process, celebrate their progress, and ultimately revel in the sense of accomplishment that accompanies crossing the finish line.

For anyone embarking on their maiden marathon voyage, this book is an indispensable companion, offering a wealth of knowledge, practical advice, and unwavering support every step of the way. With McDonnell's guidance, readers can embark on their marathon journey with confidence, knowing that they have all the tools they need to turn their aspirations into reality.

Marathon Training Strategies: A Comprehensive Guide to Running Your Best Marathon - Including Plans, Advice, and Goal-Hitting Tips

Marathon Training Strategies: A Comprehensive Guide to Running Your Best Marathon - Including Plans, Advice, and Goal-Hitting Tips

Unlock the Secrets to Marathon Success

Every step you take in the world of marathon running is a journey toward the extraordinary. The marathon is more than a race; it's a test of your willpower, endurance, and determination. To conquer the marathon and achieve your personal best, you need more than just physical strength – you need a comprehensive strategy that encompasses both body and mind. In "Marathon Training Strategies," John delves into the art and science of marathon preparation, equipping you with the knowledge, motivation, and training plans to cross the finish line in your personal best time.

Your Roadmap to Marathon Mastery

This book is not just another training guide; it's your roadmap to marathon mastery. Drawing on years of experience and expertise, John has crafted six distinct training plans, each tailored to help you reach a specific goal:

- *Sub 2:45 Marathon*: For the elite runners striving for greatness.
- *Sub 3-Hour Marathon*: An ambitious goal for those seeking to join the ranks of the sub-3 club.
- *Sub 3:15 Marathon*: A challenging yet achievable target for serious runners.
- *Sub 3:30 Marathon*: A goal that pushes the boundaries of endurance.
- *Sub 3:45 Marathon*: Perfect for runners who want to excel while balancing life's demands.
- *Sub 4-Hour Marathon*: A realistic plan for dedicated runners who want to conquer the marathon.

But "Marathon Training Strategies" is more than just training plans; it's a holistic approach to marathon preparation. He understands running a marathon isn't just about physical fitness, it's also about mental fortitude.

Your Training Companion

Within these pages, you'll discover:

Proven Training Plans: John's meticulously designed training plans are backed by science and years of experience. John's plans cater to your needs, ensuring that you're well-prepared for race day.

Nutrition and Hydration: Fueling your body is essential for marathon success. Learn how to optimize your nutrition and hydration to keep your energy levels high and your body primed for peak performance.

Injury Prevention: Running long distances can take a toll on your body. Discover effective injury prevention techniques and recovery strategies to keep you in top form throughout your training.

Mental Toughness: The marathon is as much a mental challenge as a physical one. Gain insights into visualization techniques, goal-setting strategies, and mental toughness exercises to overcome those challenging moments.

Race Day Strategies: When it comes to race day, every detail matters. From pacing and fueling to dealing with the unexpected, John guides you through the intricacies of marathon racing.

The Journey Begins Here

Whether you're aiming for a sub-2:45 marathon or striving to break the 4-hour barrier, "Marathon Training Strategies" is your trusted companion on this epic quest. It won't be easy, but it will certainly be worth it. The marathon is a test of your limits, a quest for personal excellence, and an opportunity to prove to yourself that you can achieve greatness.

"Marathon Training Strategies" is your ticket to marathon success. It's time to lace up your running shoes, set your sights on the finish line, and let this comprehensive guide be your guiding light on the path to running your best marathon ever.

Your Marathon Journey Starts Now.

Order your copy of "Marathon Training Strategies: A Comprehensive Guide to Running Your Best Marathon - Including Plans, Advice, and Goal-Hitting Tips" and unlock the secrets to marathon success today.

The "Achieve More" Running Journal: A Comprehensive Statistics Diary and Race Planner to Inspire and Help Achieve All Your Running Goals

The "Achieve More" Running Journal: A Comprehensive Statistics Diary and Race Planner to Inspire and Help Achieve All Your Running Goals is the perfect gift for any runner. It is used to track all the statistics to help inspire progress in running and fitness.

"If you can't measure it, you can't improve it." - Peter Drucker

By measuring all the vital statistics a runner needs like daily and weekly sleep, daily and weekly calorie intake, water intake, heart rate, etc., every runner will find the missing links in their running. Improvements are made easier when we see what needs to be improved. This journal tracks annual target races, running gear purchases, race entries, personal bests in every race distance.

There are templates to fill in training plans of up to 16 weeks at a time, track injuries and recoveries, and so much more:

- Sleep

- Heart Rate
- Calorie Consumption
- Water Consumption
- Trainers & Gear Purchased
- How Each Run Felt
- Weekly Summaries & Averages
- So Much More...

Make this the best running year for yourself or someone you love with this unique running journal.

APPENDIX I - BODYWEIGHT WORKOUT

Here is a bodyweight, core workout for some additional work. This will make the overall program that much easier to complete. For the first four weeks, limit this to 10 minutes per session, every day if possible. Do each of these for the number of repetitions (reps) or minutes per exercise until 10 minutes is up. In weeks five through eight, you should aim to do this same workout for 20 minutes, just looping through the workout until you hit 20 minutes.

10 x Push-ups

(if standard push-ups are too difficult, start by doing them from your knees)

20 x Crunches

Plank - 30 seconds

20 Squats

10 Dead Bugs

10 Bicycle Crunches

20 Lunges

If at any point this feels too easy, by all means, do more reps or more sets. Good technique is important in order to get the best results. You will be better off doing fewer reps with good technique and building up the quantity of reps over the weeks.

Video demonstrations of these are available on Achieve Running Club YouTube Channel

Printed in Great Britain
by Amazon